PROMISES of GOD

A Promise a day
keeps the
devil away.

Lester Sumrall

Unless otherwise indicated
all Scripture quotations are taken from
the *King James Version of the Bible.*

THE PROMISES OF GOD
ISBN 0-937580-15-5
Copyright © 1988 by Lester Sumrall
Third printing 1999
Published by Sumrall Publishing Company
P.O. Box 12
South Bend, Indiana 46624

Cover design by Paragon Communications Group

FOREWORD

There are over 7,000 promises in God's Word. The promises of God are more than food. Job 23:12, *Neither have I gone back from the commandment of his lips: I have esteemed the words of his mouth more than my necessary food.*

THE PROMISES BRING FAITH. Romans 10:8, *But what saith it? The word is nigh thee, even in thy mouth, and in thy heart: that is, the word of faith, which we preach;*

THE PROMISES BRING SPIRITUAL GROWTH. I Peter 2:2, *As newborn babes, desire the sincere milk of the word, that ye may grow thereby:*

THE PROMISES BRING REJOICING. Jeremiah 15:16, *Thy words were found, and I did eat them; and thy word was unto me the joy and rejoicing of mine heart: for I am called by thy name, O LORD God of hosts.*

THE PROMISES KEEP YOU IN CONTACT WITH GOD. Psalm 119:11, *Thy word have I hid in mine heart that I might not sin against thee.*

May this year of promises bring you joy each day. Help us win a million souls to Jesus.

JANUARY

1   *PROMISE OF COURAGE*

Fear thou not; for I am with thee: be not dismayed; for I am thy God: I will strengthen thee; yea, I will help thee.

Isaiah 41:10

The expression "FEAR NOT" is said to occur 365 times in the Bible. The cure for fear is faith in God's promises.

2   *PROMISE OF PATIENCE*

. . .We glory in tribulations also, knowing that tribulation worketh patience.

Romans 5:3

There is a lot more to the Christian life than speed. God can give you calmness amid the confusion of this world.

| 3 |

PROMISE FOR JOY

. . .For the joy of the Lord is your strength.
Nehemiah 8:10

Joy like health and peace is the condition of the Spiritual Man. It is part of the Kingdom of God. The Lord's joy can be your joy today.

| 4 |

PROMISE REGARDING LOVE

If ye keep my commandments, ye shall abide in my love. . . John 15:10

Do you love Him selfishly only for His gifts to you; or do you adore Him for His Person and presence. His presence provides sufficient gifts.

| 5 |

PROMISE OF VICTORY OVER SATAN

And they overcame him (Satan) by the blood of the Lamb. . . Revelation 12:11

Your strength and authority rests in the power

of Jesus' blood alone. Satan's oppression and work can be defeated by the blood of the Lamb. Sing it! Shout it! There is power in the blood.

6   *PROMISE FOR HEALING*

But my God shall supply all your need. . .
Philippians 4:19

Your deliverance is in the redemptive work of Christ. You can say to the Father, "In the name of Jesus I receive deliverance from this thing that has afflicted me. By the stripes of the Son of God I am healed."

7   *PROMISE TO THE RIGHTEOUS*

There is therefore now no condemnation to them which are in Christ Jesus . . .
Romans 8:1

You can become the Righteousness of God in Him (2 Cor. 5:21). Christ gives you the privilege of standing in the Father's presence as though you had never committed sin.

8 *PROMISE FOR ANSWERED PRAYER*

If I regard iniquity in my heart, the LORD will

not hear me. Psalm 66:18

Unconfessed sin constitutes a barrier between you and the Lord. Pride, selfishness, doubt, hate, etc., can be a hindrance to your prayers. Remember, He is faithful and just to forgive.

9 *PROMISE FOR WITNESSING*

Return to thine own house, and show how great things God hath done unto thee. . .

Luke 8:39

It must displease the Lord when believers fail to speak of Him to their loved ones. Witnessing, like charity, begins at home.

10 *PROMISE TO THE WEAK*

. . .God hath chosen the foolish things of the world to confound the wise. . .

I Corinthians 1:27

God delights to use the foolish things. The power of God is more fully seen when the person who uses the "sword of the Spirit" is too weak in himself to take credit for the victory.

11 *PROMISE FOR HAPPINESS*

Blessed is everyone that feareth the LORD: . . .happy shalt thou be, and it shall be well with thee.

Psalm 128:1-2

The people of the world desire happiness above everything else. They are willing to labor to find it. The Christian has found the source.

12   *PROMISE OF ESCAPE*

. . .the snare is broken, and we are escaped.

Psalm 124:7

Christ came to destroy the works of the devil, and to give deliverance to the captives. Christ is the Door. Escape for your life.

13   *PROMISE OF HIS WORD*

He sent His Word, and healed them. . .

Psalm 107:20

God sent His spoken Word through the prophets. He sent His living Word as His Son. Now He unveils the life-giving Word in the Gospels and the Epistles. He declares, ". . .The words that I have spoken unto you are spirit, and are life "(John 6:63).

14 PROMISE FOR LIFE

So teach us to number our days, that we may apply our hearts unto wisdom.

Psalm 90:12

Since we have no guarantee of tomorrow, we should treasure each hour as a jewel of great value and use it in a way that brings glory to God and blessing unto the lives of others.

15 PROMISE FOR ENDURANCE

Wait on the Lord, and keep His way . . .

Psalm 37:34

Results do not always come as rapidly as you desire. In waiting there is growth and strength often greater than the answer so impatiently longed for.

16 PROMISE OF POWER

. . .Ye shall receive power. . .and ye shall be witnesses unto me. . .

Acts 1:8

Christ empowers us through His Holy Spirit. This power is kept in force by daily prayer and Bible study. He will strengthen you today!

17   *PROMISE FOR DIRECTION*

I will instruct thee and teach thee in the way which thou shalt go: I will guide thee with mine eye.

Psalm 32:8

It is a delight to obey His command. A pilot who takes off without receiving orders may find disaster.

18   *PROMISE FOR REJOICING*

Rejoice in the Lord alway: and again I say, Rejoice.

Philippians 4:4

It is said the robin will sing in the silvery shower as well as in the bright sunshine. The believer who abides in Christ can do the same.

19   *PROMISE FOR THE HUMBLE*

He must increase, but I must decrease.

John 3:30

Our words are often more humble than our acts. Only as we are filled with the Spirit and walk in obedience to Him who was "meek and lowly in heart" will there be a decrease of self.

20   PROMISE FOR PROTECTION

The angel of the LORD encampeth round about them that fear Him, and delivereth them.

Psalm 34:7

You are just a few moments of prayer away from an angel to deliver you. Today, try and see how often He helps you in the seemingly unimportant problems.

21   PROMISE CONCERNING PRAYER

And the LORD turned the captivity of Job, when he prayed for his friends. . .

Job 42:10

Job learned praying was much more effective than arguing.

22   PROMISE FOR THE FUTURE

. . .He that doeth the will of God abideth forever.   I John 2:17

Temporal fame is like a butterfly that may be lovely to look at today, but it will be gone tomorrow. Faithful servants of God will receive a "crown of glory which fadeth not away."

23   *PROMISE FOR UNITY*

Do all things without murmurings and disputings.   Philippians 2:14

Let us use our lips for worship and reverent prayer. Our lips should SING not STING. The unity of the Spirit is lost by murmurings. David prayed, ". . .Unite my heart to fear thy name" (Psalm 86:11).

24   *PROMISE FOR THE TRUTHFUL*

Behold, thou desirest truth in the inward parts. . .   Psalm 51:6

Because the Lord is true, we should maintain the same integrity that is found in Him. A true Christian gives his word and also keeps his word.

25   *PROMISE FOR SLEEP*

. . .for so He giveth His beloved sleep.   Psalm 127:2

Lay aside every doubt and fear. Put yourself entirely in the charge of the one who has all power. "And the peace of God. . .shall keep your hearts and minds through Christ Jesus." (Philippians 4:7).

26 PROMISE FOR CHRISTIAN CHARACTER

But we. . .are changed into the same image from glory to glory. . . II Corinthians 3:18

As an heir of God and joint heir of Jesus Christ, you are to bear the image of our Lord. Your conduct and Christian character should distinguish you as a child of the King.

27 PROMISE FOR PRAYER

But when ye pray, use not vain repetitions. . .
Matthew 6:7

Prayers are only meaningful when the heart prays as well as the lips. You are better praying with your heart and without words, than praying words without your heart.

28 PROMISE REGARDING DEATH

. . .He bringeth them unto their desired haven.
Psalm 107:30

Christ has replaced the dark door of death with the beautiful gate of eternal life. He never promised us smooth sailing, just a safe landing.

29 PROMISE TO THE BELIEVER

And all things, whatsoever ye shall ask in

prayer, believing, ye shall receive.

Matthew 21:22

Refuse to look at the problems or circumstances involved; keep your eyes on the promises of God. After you have asked in faith, praise and thank God daily for the answer.

30 *PROMISE FOR RECEIVING*

. . .he that watereth shall be watered also himself. Proverbs 11:25

One of the most beautiful promises of divine government is found in the fact that no one can impart a benefit without a blessing in return.

31 *PROMISE OF HIS COMING*

Looking for that blessed hope, and the glorious appearing of. . .our Savior Jesus Christ.

Titus 2:13

From all indications, we soon shall hear the shout from on high, . . .*Well done, thou good and faithful servant. . .enter thou into the joy of the Lord* (Matthew 25:21).

FEBRUARY

1

PROMISE OF SALVATION
Being justified freely by His grace through the redemption that is in Christ Jesus.

Romans 3:24

Salvation is FREE but not CHEAP. It is the most expensive gift in the universe. He who refuses His free gift must pay the price himself with eternal death (Rom. 6:23).

2

PROMISE FOR DELIVERANCE
Cast thy burden upon the Lord, and He shall sustain thee: he shall never suffer the righteous to be moved.

Psalm 55:22

Fear, fret, anger and all other such evidences of lack of faith are destroyers. Call upon Him today. "He shall sustain thee."

3   *PROMISE FOR SERVICE*

. . .Always abounding in the work of the Lord. . .

I Corinthians 15:58

To "abound" in the work of the Lord one must go beyond the line of duty. Christians are admonished by Paul to never be satisfied with just being average. Our faithful labors are not in vain.

4   *PROMISE TO THE WEAK*

. . .ye shall be witnesses unto me. . .

Acts 1:8

Do you love to tell the story of Jesus? You can't keep quiet about the things that are really important to you. Witness for Christ with your life and your lips.

5   *PROMISE FOR THE FUTURE*

O death, where is thy sting? O grave, where

is thy victory?

I Corinthians 15:55

He who sustains you by His grace today will sustain you a million years from now in the glory of His presence. Paul said, "to be with Christ is far better."

---

6   *PROMISE TO THE PATIENT*

. . .Let patience have her perfect work, that ye may be perfect. . .

James 1:4

If our trials are borne patiently they can bring blessing and lay the foundation for future reward. Abraham was tried; he patiently waited, and received the reward.

---

7   *PROMISE FOR HEALTH AND HEALING*

And let the beauty of the Lord our God be upon us:. . .

Psalm 90:17

One essential requirement for beauty is daily sunlight. Jesus said, "I am the light." He is called the . . .*Sun of Righteousness.* . . (Mal. 4:2). His healing rays can reach you now!

8 *PROMISE FOR THE NEEDY*

Ask and it shall be given unto you. . .

Matthew 7:7

God is ready and willing to bestow what He promises upon those who in full assurance take Him at His Word and ask. We need not plead and beg God to keep His promise. He cannot lie.

9 *PROMISE FOR FAITH*

Let not your heart be troubled: . . .I go to prepare a place for you.

John 14:1-2

Feed your faith, and your doubts will starve to death.

10 *PROMISE FOR WAITING ON GOD*

Wait on the LORD: be of good courage, . . .wait, I say, on the LORD.

Psalm 27:14

The word "wait" in Psalm 27 actually means to "trust" or "hope." He will bring to fruition His plans for us. The problems of the present have already been solved by His great power.

11 PROMISE OF HIS WORD

Heaven and earth shall pass away, but my words shall not pass away.

Matthew 24:35

Christian, don't let yourself become a victim of discontent and fruitless fretting. If you do, you'll lose the peace and joy which is your rightful heritage. His comforting promises to you will not fail.

12 PROMISE FOR VICTORY

. . .we are more than conquerors through him that loved us.

Romans 8:37

We overcome in the strength of another. (I John 4:4).

13 PROMISE FOR AN ANSWER

And it shall come to pass that, before they call, I will answer;. . .

Isaiah 65:24

The Lord often makes ready in advance the help His children will require to face a crisis. Even today God's forethought is seen in the lives of His children.

14   PROMISE OF LOVE

. . .we should love one another.

I John 3:11

By the thermometer of love gauge your spirituality. Are you warm, helpful and affectionate? Or are you cold, indifferent and selfish in your attitudes?

15   PROMISE FOR PRAYER

The effectual, fervent prayer of a righteous man availeth much.

James 5:16

Words of appreciation are encouraging, but your prayers are more important than your praise.

16   PROMISE FOR THE JOURNEY

Thy shoes shall be iron and brass, and as thy days, so shall thy strength be.

Deuteronomy 33:25

If the Lord is sending you over stony paths and rough roads He provides with strong shoes.

17 PROMISE TO THE CONTENT

. . .I have learned, in whatsoever state I am, therewith to be content.

Philippians 4:11

Contentment does not depend upon things on the outside, but results from conditions on the inside.

18 PROMISE FOR BEAUTY

. . .let the beauty of the Lord our God be upon us:. . .

Psalm 90:17

As you live on the victory side of trial and test, the beauty of the Lord will increasingly radiate from your countenance.

19 PROMISE FOR THE READER

. . .give attendance to reading. . .

I Timothy 4:13

As you search for a scripture you will discover many other precious truths along the way.

20 PROMISE FOR FORGIVENESS

And their sins and iniquities will I remember

no more.   Hebrews 10:17

What a wonder of divine forgiveness. Where did our Savior bury your sins? He cannot remember!

21 *PROMISE FOR CLEANSING*

Who can understand his errors? cleanse thou me from secret faults.

Psalm 19:12

He who permits secret faults to reign undisturbed within his heart will soon be totally polluted. There can be no compromise with sin. Come to Him and say, "Cleanse thou me."

22 *PROMISE FOR STANDING*

. . .and having done all, to stand.

Ephesians 6:13

Where do you take your stand, with the crowd or with Christ? It is manlike to follow people. It is Godlike to follow principle.

23 *PROMISE OF PROVISION*

A land of wheat, and barley, and vines, and fig trees, and pomegranates; a land of oil olive,

and honey.
Deuteronomy 8:8

The foods of Egypt all grew without exception in or on the ground (onions, leeks, garlic, melons, cucumbers). In the wilderness it was manna from Heaven. When they came to Canaan the manna ceased and they fed on corn, wheat, barley, pomegranates, grapes, figs and olives. All these foods grew ABOVE the ground. They represent the believer's proper diet—heavenly things.

24   *PROMISE OF SALVATION*

. . .for he hath clothed me with the garments of salvation, he hath covered me with the robe of righteousness,. . .
Isaiah 61:10

No matter how carefully tailored, man's best efforts are only inadequate "fig leaves."

25   *PROMISE FOR PRAYER*

. . .when thou hast shut thy door, pray. . .
Matthew 6:6

After the disciples witnessed the prayer-life of

Jesus they came to Him and said, . . .*Lord, teach us to pray.* . . (Luke 11:1).

26 PROMISE TO FRIENDS

I thank my God upon every remembrance of you.

Philippians 1:3

Does anyone praise the Lord for the blessing of your friendship? Friendship brings intimate joys of mutual help and understanding. You can never replace a friend, each one is pleasingly different.

27 PROMISE TO THE UNFORGIVING

Grudge not one against another, brethren. . .

James 5:9

To carry a grudge will hurt no one else as much as it will hurt you. If you carry a grudge it is because you will not forgive. What if God carried a grudge against us?

28 PROMISE OF HIS LEADING

. . .*use not liberty for an occasion to the flesh, but by love serve one another.*

Galatians 5:13

Freedom from the law does not give us the right to do as we please, but opens the door to Christ who leads us to do as we ought.

29   *PROMISE OF HIS COMING*

But of that day and hour knoweth no man. . .

Matthew 24:36

God doesn't want us to become preoccupied with specific future dates. He wants us to live in fellowship with Him right now. The fact of His coming does not depend on our knowing when.

$\mathcal{M}$ARCH

1
PROMISE OF SAFETY

. . .in the shadow of thy wings will I re-joice. . .thy right hand upholdeth me.

Psalm 63:7-8

Safety is not the absence of danger, but the presence of God.

2
PROMISE OF SALVATION

. . .Believe on the Lord Jesus Christ, and thou shalt be saved, . . .

Acts 16:31

Have you been depending on your efforts to get to Heaven? We must simply commit ourselves to the Savior, relying on Him, and Him alone.

3   *PROMISE TO THE HUMBLE*

Humble yourselves therefore under the mighty hand of God, that He may exalt you in due time.

I Peter 5:6

Humility is a possession you lose the moment you think you've really got it.

4   *PROMISE FOR VICTORY*

Set your affection on things above, not on things on the earth.

Colossians 3:2

Remember, sinful appetites cannot survive in great spiritual heights.

5   *PROMISE FOR REST*

Rest in the Lord, and wait patiently for him. . .

Psalm 37:7

Relax by trusting the One who "*. . .is able to make all grace abound toward you. . .*"

(II Cor. 9:8).

6 *PROMISE IN TIME OF TROUBLE*

. . .I will be with him in trouble. . .

Psalm 91:15

He has not promised to keep us OUT of trouble, but He does promise "I will be with him IN trouble."

7 *PROMISE FOR THOSE WHO PRAY*

The eyes of the Lord are upon the righteous, and His ears are open unto their cry.

Psalm 34:15

Praying is to the soul what breathing is to the body. "Pray without ceasing" (I Thes. 5:17).

8 *PROMISE TO THE OVERTAKEN*

. . .if a man be overtaken in a fault,. . .restore such an one in the spirit of meekness;. . .

Galatians 6:1

There is a great difference between being overtaken in a fault and deliberately sinning.

9 *PROMISE FOR FAITH*

So then faith cometh by hearing, and hearing by the Word of God.

Romans 10:17

The Holy Spirit never witnesses with our spirit outside of His Word. We should be more concerned about hearing the Lord, than the Lord hearing us.

10 — PROMISE FOR HEALING

. . .but be ye transformed by the renewing of your mind,. . .

Romans 12:2

The renewed mind will praise the Father that our diseases were laid on Christ and He put them away. I am healed by the power of the Son of God. I thank the Father that it is done.

11 — PROMISE FOR SPIRITUAL GROWTH

. . .and every branch that beareth fruit, he purgeth it, that it may bring forth more fruit.

John 15:2

The pruning knife is the Word of God which is sharp and powerful. Those fit for His service He desires to make more fit.

12 — PROMISE FOR THE WEARY

But ye, brethren, be not weary in well doing.

II Thessalonians 3:13

Find out your special job and do it faithfully, even if no one else notices it.

13   *PROMISE FOR GIVING*

Honour the LORD with thy substance, and with the firstfruits of all thine increase: So shall thy barns be filled with plenty, and thy presses shall burst out with new wine.

Proverbs 3:9-10

Heaven has a record of that poor widow who truly gave more than all the rich men together (Mark 12:43).

14   *PROMISE FOR LIFE*

For whoso findeth Me findeth life, and shall obtain favour of the Lord.

Proverbs 8:35

Eternal "life" and divine "favor" are beautiful virtues from the Lord.

15   *PROMISE TO THE BODY*

But now hath God set the members every one of them in the body, as it hath pleased Him.

I Corinthians 12:18

In the church today we see some artificial limbs. They do not have any feeling in them.

16 PROMISE AGAINST SIN

When the Heaven is shut up, and there is no rain, because they have sinned against Thee...

II Chronicles 6:26

A silent and irresponsive Heaven is a fearful calamity to a needy soul. Heaven is still shut up to the disobedient and the backsliding. To those who repent the Heavens will open!

17 PROMISE OVER FEAR

. . .Fear not: for they that be with us are more than they that be with them.

II Kings 6:16

Remember we are not alone and deserted even when we seem most to be.

18 PROMISE FOR A DOUBLE PORTION

. . .let a double portion of thy spirit be upon me.

II Kings 2:9

Elisha loved to be with his master, now he seeks to be like him.

19 PROMISE FOR PEACE

Peace I leave with you, my peace I give unto you. . .

John 14:27

The word can say, "Peace!" but can do nothing to give it. When Jesus says, "Peace," the power of Heaven is ever present to bestow peace.

20 PROMISE TO GLORIFY GOD

. . .immediately she. . .glorified God.

Luke 13:13

Her feet were taken out of the horrible pit of her eighteen years' bondage. The snare was broken by the power of the Savior.

21 PROMISE OF HEALING

He sent His Word and healed them, and delivered them from their destructions.

Psalm 107:20

God's healing powers rescue life from death and destruction.

22 PROMISE OF HONOR

His work is honourable and glorious. . .

Psalm 111:3

33

The Lord is holy in all His works. There is dignity in the work of Creation and Redemption that honors our God.

| 23 | **PROMISE OF DEDICATION** |

I will keep thy statutes. . .

Psalm 119:8

The heart that is right with God will be attentive to His Words.

| 24 | **PROMISE OF LIVING WATER** |

. . .the waters gushed out, and the streams overflowed. . .

Psalm 78:20

The supply is still abundant. "Whosoever will may come and take of the water of life freely" (Revelation 22:17).

| 25 | **PROMISE FOR REPENTANCE** |

If we confess our sins, He is faithful and just to forgive us our sins. . .

I John 1:9

Sins that are not confessed prevent us from experiencing the light of God's grace in our hearts. Even those around us will sense that something is wrong.

26 PROMISE FOR LEADING

For that ye ought to say, If the Lord will, we shall live, and do this, or that.

James 4:15

Such a life of complete reliance upon His leading is not only blessed but BEST!

27 PROMISE TO THE BELIEVER

. . .all things work together for good to them that love God,. . . Romans 8:28

The unsaved have no such promise! Even the blessing they are now receiving will eventually cry out against them in the day of judgment.

28 PROMISE FOR CLEANSING

Woe unto you, scribes and Pharisees, hypocrites! For ye are like unto whited sepulchers,. . . Matthew 23:27

Many religious leaders of Jesus' day were sanctimonious hypocrites who trusted in themselves that they were righteous. No matter how much you whitewash yourself or stand firm in your own righteousness, only Christ can wash you white and cleanse you from sin.

29 PROMISE OF VICTORY OVER SATAN

Submit yourselves therefore to God. Resist the devil, and he will flee from you.

James 4:7

The devil was defeated at Calvary and has no right in your life. Tell him he is on God's property, and demand that he depart.

30 PROMISE OF THE COMFORTER

. . .I will pray the Father, and he shall give you another Comforter. . . John 14:16

At Pentecost the Savior kept that promise. As Comforter He will stand with us in difficulty. He will not be a party to anything that would promote sin or deception. His Spirit will aid us only in truth and holiness.

31 PROMISE FOR HOPE

And in the fourth watch of the night Jesus went into them, walking on the sea.

Matthew 14:25

Jesus comes to you bringing hope to help you stand in the face of your storm.

$\mathcal{A}$PRIL

1 PROMISE OF REFRESHING

There is a river, the streams whereof shall make glad the city of God. . .

Psalm 46:4

Rivers of delight flow out for the soul that has found its refuge in God. There are living streams of eternal truth.

2 PROMISE OF FAITHFULNESS

They (the Lord's mercies) are new every morning: great is thy faithfulness.

Lamentations 3:23

His manna of blessing must be regularly appropriated. Each day there are new mercies to delight our seeking souls.

3

PROMISE FOR TRUTH

Howbeit when He, the Spirit of truth, is come, He will guide you into all truth:. . .

John 16:13

If you are searching for the Truth as it is in Jesus, receive the guidance of His heavenly Helper, the Holy Spirit.

4

PROMISE TO THE MEEK

The meek shall eat and be satisfied. . .

Psalm 22:26

We are told in the Scripture, the meek shall be guided by God (Psa. 25:9); beautified with salvation (Psa. 149:4); taught of the Lord (Psa. 25:9); inherit the earth (Matt. 5:5); and be greatly treasured by the Lord (I Peter 3:4).

5

PROMISE FOR PROTECTION

I bare you on eagles' wings. . .Exodus 19:4.
. . .how often would I have gathered thy children together, even as a hen gathereth her

chickens under her wings. . .

Matthew 23:37
In the Old Testament you are seen on the wings, but in the New Testament God hides us under His wings. Which is the safer of the two "on" or "under"? There is no position so near to the heart of God, as under His wing.

6 PROMISE FOR THOSE WHO CALL

Call unto me, and I will answer thee, and shew thee great and mighty things, which thou knowest not.

Jeremiah 33:3
All power in heaven and earth is under God's control. He is waiting for your call, He will answer in miraculous ways.

7 PROMISE TO THE CHURCH

. . .I will build my church; and the gates of hell shall not prevail against it.

Matthew 16:18
The true church has been guaranteed not only survival but success. Its future is secure in the Rock of Ages.

8   PROMISE OF JOY

Be glad in the Lord, and rejoice, ye righteous: and shout for joy, all ye that are upright in heart.

Psalm 32:11

It is a blessed experience to leave the doubters and join the shouters.

9   PROMISE FOR ALL CHRISTIANS

. . .what is that to thee? follow thou Me.

John 21:22

While others seem to have the easy road, may these words of the Lord Jesus ring in our ears. Your responsibility is to be faithful to your calling.

10   PROMISE OF GRACE

. . .Whosoever will come after me, let him deny himself,. . .

Mark 8:34

Grace is given only to the humble. Pride must be crucified.

11 · PROMISE FOR FAITH

. . .faith cometh by hearing, and hearing by the Word of God.

Romans 10:17

Faith is believing that God will do for, in, or through you what He promises in His Word. For strong faith, hear and believe the Word of God.

12 · PROMISE FOR SERVICE

There is a lad here, which hath five barley loaves, and two small fishes: but what are they among so many?

John 6:9

If you are one of God's little ones and feel your efforts are almost useless, remember it is not the amount you have, it is what Jesus can do with whatever you have to offer Him.

13 · PROMISE OF REDEMPTION

. . .It is finished. . .   John 19:30

Jesus not only said it was finished but He arose to PROVE it! When He stepped forth as the Victor over the grave, the debt was paid. Redemption is FINISHED!

41

14   *PROMISE FOR TRIALS*

My brethren, count it all joy when ye fall into divers temptations (various trials).

James 1:2

Count your troubles and testings as "JOY!" Difficulties can become opportunities with Christ dwelling in you.

15   *PROMISE OF LIFE*

. . .I am come that they might have life. . .

John 10:10

The woman who touched the hem of His garment received life abundantly. In Him there is all-sufficiency to satisfy.

16   *PROMISE OF REST*

And he (Jesus) said unto them, come. . .apart into a desert place, and rest a while:. . .

Mark 6:31

The Lord sometimes calls us apart to worship, to evaluate our spiritual status, and to generate the power needed for the days ahead. There is a time for resting as well as working.

17 PROMISE FOR GOOD

. . .No good thing will He withhold from them that walk uprightly.

Psalm 84:11

Do not be rebellious when God refuses your requests. The thing you think you cannot live without at the moment, may not be for your good in the future. If you knew the future you would thank Him for denying you that for which you now so tearfully plead. He never withholds anything that is truly "good."

18 PROMISE FOR SAFETY

I will both lay me down in peace, and sleep; for thou, Lord, only makest me dwell in safety.

Psalm 4:8

By placing your trust in the Lord, you can close your eyes in sleep with the assurance that the problems of tomorrow will not be greater than the God of eternity. The Christian can know, whether he dies before he wakes or wakes before he dies, all is well.

19 PROMISE OF RECEIVING

But let him ask in faith, nothing wavering. For

he that wavereth is like a wave of the sea driven
with the wind and tossed.

James 1:6

There is no stability about a wave; it is utterly
purposeless, being driven about with the wind.
"All things whatsoever ye ask in prayer, believing, ye shall receive" (Matthew 21:22).

20   PROMISE FOR THE FUTURE

For I am the Lord, I change not;. . .

Malachi 3:6

If God were moved by any whim or sudden
notion, our eternal destiny would be constantly
in jeopardy. Things on earth may change, but
God and His Word stand sure.

21   PROMISE TO DELIVER

And call upon me in the day of trouble: I will
deliver thee, and thou shalt glorify me.

Psalm 50:15

You may know this day that God will hear the
cries of His own. He will deliver and praises
thou shalt give to Him.

22   PROMISE FOR CLEANSING

. . .if we walk in the light. . .the blood of Jesus

Christ His Son cleanseth us from all sin.
I John 1:7

You will never overcome the besetting sins of this life in your own strength. New evils will crop up as fast as the old ones are defeated. Only as you walk in the light of the Father and the Son, can you maintain spiritual victory.

23   *PROMISE OF A SONG*

Yet. . .in the night His song shall be with me. . .
Psalm 42:8

Though the night of trial settles dark on every hand, yet through the power of the Holy Spirit there is a song in the night.

24   *PROMISE FOR WINNING THE RACE*

. . .let us lay aside every weight, and. . . run. . .the race. . .looking unto Jesus. . .
Hebrews 12:1-2

Too many Christains spend time in vain regrets over past failures. If you look at yourself you will be discouraged, look at others and you will be defeated, look to Christ and you will be victorious!

25 | PROMISE FOR THE WEEPING

They that sow in tears shall reap in joy.
                                    Psalm 126:5

Tears are often used by the Lord to soften the ground of the heart to better receive the precious seed of the Word of God.

26 | PROMISE FOR THE FAITHFUL

Keep yourselves in the love of God. . .
                                    Jude 21

Let the "Sun of Righteousness" shine upon you. It is the fruit ripened in the sun that is the sweetest. Never stay sullenly in the shadows.

27 | PROMISE OF SALVATION

. . .we shall be saved by His life.
                                    Romans 5:10

He died to save us; He lives to keep us saved.

28 | PROMISE FOR GIVING

Give, and it shall be given unto you; good measure. . .and running over, . . .
                                    Luke 6:38

The more you shovel out, the more the Lord will shovel in. Be sure of this, the Lord's shovel is bigger than yours.

29 PROMISE TO REMEMBER

. . .this do in remembrance of me.

I Corinthians 11:24

The word "remember" occurs in various forms more than 200 times in the Bible. He intends for us to be encouraged by past blessings and answers to prayer.

30 PROMISE CONCERNING PRAYER

. . .The effectual fervent prayer of a righteous man availeth much.

James 5:16

Elijah was not afraid to continue asking God for the thing needed, for his prayer for rain was made seven times before the answer came.

MAY

1   *PROMISE FOR DECISION*

. . .the town clerk. . . .said,. . .ye ought to be quiet, and to do nothing rashly.
          Acts 19:35-36

If you are facing a difficult decision, don't react hurriedly. Hurry produces many mistakes. Remember the town clerk who advised, "Do nothing rashly!"

2   *PROMISE OF STRENGTH*

He delivered me from my strong enemy, . . .
          Psalm 18:17

Your adversary, the devil, is a strong enemy, but One stronger than he has come to seek and to save (Luke 19:10).

3 ## PROMISE OF HOLINESS

In that day shall there be upon the bells of the horses, HOLINESS UNTO THE LORD. . .

Zechariah 14:20

There are many kinds of bells: wedding bells, cowbells, dumbbells, etc. Let's ring the bells that ring, "HOLINESS UNTO THE LORD!"

4 ## PROMISE TO BE SPIRIT FILLED

And be not drunk with wine, wherein is excess; but be filled with the Spirit;

Ephesians 5:18

Stop trying to empty your problems through sheer willpower; let Bible study, prayer and worship fill you. When the Holy Spirit fills you there is no room for the wrong things.

5 ## PROMISE FOR HEALING

. . .for I am the Lord that healeth thee.

Exodus 15:26

You are under the decree of God that releases you from the law of sin and death. God's Word is a light that reduces your darkness to nothingness.

6 | PROMISE TO THE DISCOURAGED

Though he fall, he shall not be utterly cast down. . .

Psalm 37:24

Are you down this morning? There is something worse than being down—it is staying down. Confess your need of His strength. His provision can reach you now.

7 | PROMISE TO THE BRIDE OF CHRIST

And he saith. . .Friend, how camest thou in hither not having a wedding garment?. . .

Matthew 22:12

Only those arrayed in His righteousness can find acceptance with God. You will never make it if you're dressed in the wrong clothes!

8 | PROMISE FOR THE SUFFERING

But the God of all grace,. . .after that ye have suffered a while,. . .strengthen, settle you.

I Peter 5:10

God often uses difficult circumstances to develop maturity in our lives. Have you noticed that many noble saints of God have had to face severe hardship and persecution?

| **9** |

PROMISE OF BLESSINGS

. . .For all things are yours. . .and ye are Christ's. . .

I Corinthians 3:21, 23

The redeemed soul is overwhelmed because of all the divine blessings given to us. We are spiritual millionaires in Christ!

| **10** |

PROMISE OF DELIVERANCE

. . .thy rod and thy staff they comfort me.

Psalm 23:4

The club and the crook of the shepherd were the instruments of defence and deliverance. Our shepherd will beat off our enemies, or lift those who have fallen into a pit or ditch.

| **11** |

PROMISE FOR GOD'S WILL

Present your bodies a living sacrifice, holy, acceptable unto God, . . .

Romans 12:1

Many are answering the call to have Christ save

their souls but selfishly reserve their bodies for their own purposes and enjoyment. This keeps the believer from knowing the perfect will of God (Romans 12:1).

12 *PROMISE OF HIS SPIRIT*

. . .my Spirit remaineth among you: fear ye not.

Haggai 2:5

To know His presence remaineth among you is a great source of cheer and strength.

13 *PROMISE FOR WORK*

. . .for the people had a mind to work.

Nehemiah 4:6

They did not have a mind to sit moping over their difficulties, or to spend their time in mere talk or faultfinding.

14 *PROMISE OF FAITH*

And when He saw their faith, He said. . .

Luke 5:20

When He sees your unwavering trust, He will act! Exercise your faith this day that it may grow stronger.

15 | PROMISE TO HIS LITTLE FLOCK

Fear not, little flock; for it is your Father's good pleasure to give you the kingdom.

Luke 12:32

The flock may be little, but the pleasure of the Father-Shepherd towards them is VERY GOOD.

16 | PROMISE FOR LIFE AND PEACE

. . .not I, but Christ. . .

Galatians 2:20

Self is carnal, Christ is spiritual. "For to be carnally minded is death; but to be spiritually minded is life and peace" (Romans 8:6).

17 | PROMISE FOR PRAYER

. . .He spake. . .unto them to this end, that men ought always to pray, and not to faint;

Luke 18:1

There are five examples of prayer in this chapter: a widow, a Pharisee, a publican, a ruler and a beggar. All men ought to pray.

PROMISE OF WARNING

. . .this night thy soul shall be required of thee. . .

Luke 12:20

Death to the unsaved rich is their bill of bankruptcy while they are dreaming of plenty. Those who live for their own good can never receive the Master's "Well done."

19

PROMISE OF GOD'S WORD

The statutes of the Lord are. . .more to be desired. . .than gold, yea, than much fine gold. . .

Psalm 19:8, 10

Growth in the Christian life is determined by the value one places upon the Bible. The Lord Himself has exalted His Word above His name (Psalm 138:2). A tremendous amount of spiritual wealth is contained in a single copy of the Scriptures.

20

PROMISE FOR BOLDNESS

I will speak of Thy testimonies. . .and will not be ashamed.

Psalm 119:46

This was true of the Apostle Paul, ". . .I am not ashamed of the Gospel of Christ. . ." (Romans 1:16).

21 PROMISE FOR THE MIDNIGHT HOUR

At midnight I will rise to give thanks unto Thee. . .

Psalm 119:62

Blessed are all they who can rise up in the midnight hour of their sorrow and gloom, and give thanks unto the Lord.

22 PROMISE FOR TRUST

What time I am afraid, I will trust in Thee.

Psalm 56:3

It is a blessed fear that frightens us to God. "I will" is the confession that removes the doubt.

23 PROMISE CONCERNING SIN

He that covereth his sins shall not prosper: . . .

Proverbs 28:13

. . .Charity shall cover the multitude of sins.

I Peter 4:8

Most people cover their own sin, and uncover the sins of others. These Scriptures declare you should cover a multitude of sins of others, but uncover your own sin (I John 1:9).

24 | PROMISE OF PARADISE

. . .To day shalt thou be with me in paradise.

Luke 23:43

The penitent thief was the first to enter paradise through the blood of the Lamb.

25 | PROMISE FOR SERVICE

And now send. . .to Joppa, and call for. . .Peter.

Acts 10:5

God could have sent His angel to Cornelius, but He chooses redeemed ones to work with Him.

26 | PROMISE FOR ENTHUSIASM

And Philip ran thither to him. . .

Acts 8:30

Real enthusiasm in the work of God is a rare accomplishment in these last days.

27 PROMISE CONCERNING POWER

. . .and when the man was let down, and touched the bones of Elisha, he revived, and stood up on his feet.

II Kings 13:21

There is power in the dead bones of a MAN OF GOD!

28 PROMISE FOR THE RACE

. . .let us run. . .the race. . .

Hebrews 12:1

A man in a race is always wide awake. There must be continuance in well doing in order to be a winner. (Romans 2:7)

29 PROMISE OF PENTECOST

Then Peter said, Silver and gold have I none; but such as I have give I thee. . .

Acts 3:6

They had neither "silver nor gold," but they had something better. They had the power of Calvary and Pentecost.

30 PROMISE TO THE WEAK

Be not deceived; God is not mocked. . .

Galatians 6:7

In matters of religion how many are only masquerading. Many love to disguise themselves that they may participate in some new pleasure which they could not have without the mask.

31 PROMISE TO THE FAITHFUL

. . .be thou faithful unto death, and I will give thee a crown of life.

Revelation 2:10

Remember it is not success that God rewards, it is faithfulness.

JUNE

1 | PROMISE OF LIFE

. . .I am come that they might have life
. . .more abundantly.

John 10:10

The tree that is not rooted will become fruitless. Fruit is not for the good of the tree, it is the good of the tree.

2 | PROMISE OF LEARNING

Take my yoke upon you, and learn of Me;...

Matthew 11:29

To learn of Christ we must get close to Him.

3   *PROMISE TO THE BRIDE*

And the Spirit and the bride say, Come. . .
Revelation 22:17

In this the Spirit and the bride are co-workers, inviting the "bright and Morning Star" (vs.16).

4   *PROMISE FOR THE SEARCHING*

And ye shall seek Me, and find Me, when ye shall search for Me with all your heart.
Jeremiah 29:13

There is plenty of room on the broad way that leads to destruction. There is room for all the sinner's likes and pleasures. Before you is set the way of life and the way of death (Jer. 21:8). Choose life.

5   *PROMISE OF AN OPEN DOOR*

. . .behold, I have set before thee an open door,. . .
Revelation 3:8

Thank God it is the "front door!" There are no back doors into the Kingdom of God. (John 14:6)

6 PROMISE CONCERNING PRAISE

*And when they began to sing and to praise,
. . .they (the enemy) were smitten.*

II Chronicles 20:22

Jehoshaphat appointed a choir to go before the army. As they began "to sing and to praise," Judah gained a great victory. The people didn't lift a finger to fight. The conquering power of praise to God had won the battle.

7 PROMISE OF POWER

. . .tarry ye. . .until ye be endued with power. . .

Luke 24:49

No use going without it. David had to wait for the moving in the trees before he could stir. If he stirred before the moving he stirred without God (II Samuel 5:24).

8 PROMISE OVER STORMS

. . .And when Peter was come down out of the ship, he walked on the water, to go to Jesus.

Matthew 14:29

You can walk on the most deadly storm you have ever encountered if your eyes are on Jesus.

9   *PROMISE FOR ETERNAL LIFE*

. . .I will come again, and receive you unto Myself; that where I am, there ye may be also.

John 14:3

He will keep His promise and we shall soon dwell with Him in glory. Cheer up, the best is yet to come.

10   *PROMISE FOR FAITH*

. . .I say unto you, I have not found so great faith, no, not in Israel.

Matthew 8:10

Great faith lays hold on the greatness of Christ.

11   *PROMISE OF MERCY*

. . .he shall eat at my table, as one of the king's sons.

II Samuel 9:11

Mephibosheth was lame in both feet because of a fall. God's table of mercy covers all infirmity.

12   *PROMISE FOR HEALING*

He healeth the broken in heart, and bindeth

up their wounds.
Psalm 147:3

Disease came with the fall, and sickness is a work of the adversary. Because disease came with the fall, God is the logical Healer. He is honored by our acting on His Word. He watches over it to make it good.

13 *PROMISE FOR WISDOM*

. . .Ye men of Athens,. . .
Acts 17:22

No preacher ever addressed a more critical congregation. The wisdom of God is greater than man's wisdom.

14 *PROMISE FOR PEACE*

And let the peace of God rule in your hearts,. . .and be ye thankful.
Colossians 3:15

His yoke is easy. His burden is light. Be thankful that He is able, that His grace is sufficient, that He never fails.

15 *PROMISE OF BLESSING*

The Lord is my Shepherd; I shall not want.
Psalm 23:1

Beneath me, "green pastures." Beside me, "still waters." Before me, "a table." Upon me, "anointing." Following me, "goodness and mercy." Beyond me, "the house of the Lord for ever" (Psalm 23).

16 PROMISE FOR SERVICE

. . .for the people had a mind to work.
Nehemiah 4:6

The greatest defect in all branches of Christian service is laziness. Work while it is TODAY!

17 PROMISE FOR PROVISION

. . .good measure, pressed down, and shaken together, and running over. . .
Luke 6:38

What man produces is like the box of cereal, "spread out, blown up and half full." God always gives a fair portion.

18 PROMISE OF DELIVERANCE

. . .I know of a surety, that the Lord hath sent His angel, and hath delivered me. . .
Acts 12:11

No conqueror ever had a more triumphant march than Peter had from the state prison to Prayer Meeting Street.

19 *PROMISE OF SALVATION*

. . .for it is the power of God. . .

Romans 1:16

Salvation has been a more costly work to God than creation.

20 *PROMISE TO HELP*

. . .the Spirit. . .helpeth our infirmities:. . . He maketh intercession for the saints according to the will of God.

Romans 8: 26-27

The Holy Spirit does not help our SINS, but He does help our INFIRMITIES!

21 *PROMISE TO HIS CHURCH*

. . .upon this Rock I will build My church;. . .

Matthew 16:18

We need to give the Church back to Jesus; He will build it.

22 *PROMISE OF GREAT UNDERSTANDING*

He that is slow to wrath is of great understand-

ing: but he that is hasty of spirit exalteth folly.
Proverbs 14:29

Have you heard the expression "cool as a cucumber?" The center of a cucumber is always much cooler than the outer rind and the atmosphere surrounding it. Let's learn a lesson and abide in the vine.

23   *PROMISE FOR VICTORY*

. . .greater is He that is in you, than he that is in the world.
I John 4:4

". . . we wrestle not against flesh and blood, but against principalities,. . .powers,. . .the rulers of the darkness of this world,. . ." (Eph. 6:12). Our warfare must be in the power of the Holy Spirit, or it will be unavailing.

24   *PROMISE OF HIS WORD*

. . .My Word. . .shall accomplish that which I please,. . .
Isaiah 55:11

His Word went forth in creation and turned emptiness into fruitfulness. Be assured that it will accomplish that which is pleasing unto God. His Word shall never pass away (Matthew 24:35).

25   *PROMISE OF LIVING WATER*

. . .the water that I shall give him shall be in him a well of water springing up. . .

John 4:14

Cleansing must precede usefulness. The well is deep, for the source is our God.

26   *PROMISE OF THE NEW BIRTH*

And you hath He quickened, who were dead in trespasses and sins.

Ephesians 2:1

The dead have nothing in common with the living. They are repulsive, and unfit for fellowship. While we were in our sins we were out of communion with God. By the new birth we are "alive unto God."

27   *PROMISE OF BLESSING*

As an eagle stirreth up her nest. . .So the Lord. . .did lead him. . .

Deuteronomy 32:11-12

The soft down of contentment is often removed from our earthly nests so that we may spread our wings of faith, and soar to new heights of blessing.

28 PROMISE FOR THE REPENTANT

And they went out, and preached that men should repent.

Mark 6:12

Mere sorrow for sin cannot lessen the guilt. Real repentance is a necessity (Acts 17:30). Try a repentance that needs not to be repented of.

29 PROMISE FOR JOY

Then was our mouth filled with laughter. . .
Psalm 126:2

Laughter is a wonderful gift from God. It is a releasing of tension. Make sure your laughter is the right kind. Let it be an expression of a pure mind. Remember, the Savior brings great joy.

30 PROMISE IN DISAPPOINTMENT

. . .I am like a broken vessel.

Psalm 31:12

Men's disappointments are ever God's appointments.

*J*ULY

1

PROMISE FOR FAITH

Beloved, think it not strange concerning the fiery trial which is to try you,. . . .But rejoice,. . .

I Peter 4:12-13

Some Christians think it strange when they have a fiery trial. You cannot determine the strength of a rope until tension is applied to it. You will never know how strong your faith is until it is tested.

2

PROMISE TO THE HUMBLE

. . .he that shall humble himself shall be exalted.

Matthew 23:12

69

We must humble ourselves to experience His fullest and best. The smaller we become, the more room God has for His blessings.

3　　PROMISE TO THE WEAK

. . .be content with such things as ye have. . .
Hebrews 13:5

Happiness does not consist in the abundance of things we possess, it is the appreciation of the things we do possess. The grass is NOT always greener on the other side of the fence.

4　　PROMISE FOR FREEDOM

If the Son therefore shall make you free, ye shall be free indeed.
John 8:36

He not only will set you free from your oppression, He will remove the chains that had you bound so you can follow Him.

5　　PROMISE FOR AN ANSWER

. . .And he said, I will not let thee go, except thou bless me.
Genesis 32:26

Now that his strength is broken, Jacob the resister becomes the clinger. This cry of entire dependence is always sure to bring an answer.

6 | PROMISE OF HIS WORD

. . .I will fear no evil: . . .   Psalm 23:4

Our joy of the Lord depends on our knowledge of the absolute certainty of the promises of God.

7 | PROMISE OF THE KINGDOM

Fear not,. . .for it is your Father's good pleasure to give you the kingdom. Luke 12:32

". . .My kingdom is not of this world: . . ." said Christ (John 18:36). The things of the earth shall pass away but the kingdom of God "cannot be moved" (Hebrews 12:28).

8 | PROMISE OF FAITH

. . .According to your faith be it unto you.

Matthew 9:29

God cannot honour distrust, for distrust dishonours God.

9 | PROMISE OF RICHES

And I will give thee. . .hidden riches of secret places,. ..

Isaiah 45:3

"In whom (Him) are hid all the treasures of wisdom and knowledge." (Colossians 2:3)

10   PROMISE OF SEPARATION

. . .Lot dwelled in the cities of the plain, and pitched his tent toward Sodom.
           Genesis 13:12

Those who walk by sight and not by faith will always be influenced by appearances. Mixing with the world often means helping the ungodly.

11   PROMISE FOR PROVISION

Whether. . .things present, or things to come; all are yours.
           I Corinthians 3:22

We are joint-heirs with Christ in all things. We may have to wait to receive our full abundant inheritance, but there is much we can claim today.

12   PROMISE FOR PRAYER

. . .God forbid that I should sin against the Lord in ceasing to pray for you:. . .
           I Samuel 12:23

Prayer is a wonderful service for God and your fellow man though it seldom calls for the praise of men.

13 | PROMISE OF VICTORY

And take. . .the sword of the Spirit, which is the word of God.

Ephesians 6:17

When we hear and obey God, we will walk in victory every day.

14 | PROMISE IN TRIBULATION

. . .In the world ye shall have tribulation: but be of good cheer; I have overcome the world.

John 16:33

There are two ways of meeting inevitable troubles. We can give up, lose heart, become bitter and complaining, or we can be of good cheer, face them in faith, believing that our Father has a wise purpose in it all.

15 | PROMISE FOR THE BROKENHEARTED

The Lord is nigh unto them that are of a broken heart;. . .

Psalm 34:18

It is a dark day when your heart is broken, but God is there. He is nigh; call on Him. He is so nigh a whisper will bring a response.

16 | PROMISE FOR CONTENTMENT

. . .it pleased God by the foolishness of

preaching to save them that believe.
I Corinthians 1:21

The foolishness of preaching is not foolish preaching.

17 PROMISE FOR CONTENTMENT

But godliness with contentment is great gain.
I Timothy 6:6

In this life you will meet some poor rich folks, and you will meet some rich poor folks. We all live in one of two tents: CON-TENT or DISCON-TENT.

18 PROMISE OF EVERLASTING LIFE

Enter ye in at the strait gate:. . .
Matthew 7:13

The way may be strait, but, thank God, it is not shut.

19 PROMISE WITH CONDITION

Then I will give you rain in the due season, and . . . fruit. . .
Leviticus 26:4

"Then," you see this promise is conditional. Fruitfulness depends on our relationship to God.

20   *PROMISE FOR THE LORD'S SUPPER*

. . .Jesus took bread, and blessed, and brake it, and gave to them, and said, Take, eat: this is My body.

Mark 14:22

The acts of Jesus are as significant as His words. In observing the Lord's Supper we are called to remember Him as our SACRIFICE, to show forth His death till He comes.

21   *PROMISE OF SIMPLICITY*

. . .except ye be converted, and become as little children, ye shall not enter into the kingdom of heaven.

Matthew 18:3

"A little child." Not a little boy who thinks himself a man. For many there is a big step down (or up) into the honest simplicity of a trustful child.

22   *PROMISE OF REFUGE*

And let us arise, and go up to Bethel;. . .

Genesis 35:3

Jacob had forgotten his covenant with God; God had not forgotten His promise to Jacob.

Our gracious God still reminds us of the place of refuge for our troubled souls.

23   *PROMISE OF BLESSING*

. . .that signs and wonders may be done by the Name of thy holy child Jesus.

Acts 4:30

Our self-sufficiency will always paralyze the wonderworking hand of the Holy Spirit.

24   *PROMISE FOR HEALING*

For I will restore health unto thee, and I will heal thee of thy wounds, saith the Lord;...

Jeremiah 30:17

The power of God manifested in healing is never failing. Give yourself to Him body, mind and spirit. He will keep His Word.

25   *PROMISE TO HIS SHEEP*

The Lord is my Shepherd. . .

Psalm 23:1

Sheep have no means of defense. Their only safety lies in the power and care of the shepherd. "My sheep hear My voice, and I know them, and they follow Me. . .neither shall any man pluck them out of My hand." (John 10:27-28).

26 PROMISE OF PROTECTION

. . .yea, in the shadow of Thy wings will I make my refuge,. . .

Psalm 57:1

The best protection in time and eternity is the fallout shelter of "feathers." "He shall cover thee with His feathers, and under His wings shalt thou trust:. . ." (Psalm 91:4).

27 PROMISE OF JUDGMENT

For by thy words thou shalt be justified, and by thy words thou shalt be condemned.

Matthew 12:37

Does your conversation reveal that you are a disciple of Christ? You will notice a short intellect usually has a long tongue.

28 PROMISE CONCERNING THE SPIRIT

. . .the LORD stirred up the spirit of Cyrus. . .

Ezra 1:1

Cold, mechanical service is an insult to the living God. The will of God will never be done until the spirit within us is stirred.

29   ## *PROMISE OF WARNING*

Love not the world, neither the things that are in the world. If any man love the world, the love of the Father is not in him.
        I John 2:15

Love for the evil world system with its greed, selfishness, ambition and pleasure cancels out love for God. Some folks have Heaven on their tongue, but the world in their hand.

30   ## *PROMISE FOR A NEW HEART*

And a certain woman named Lydia,. . .heard us: whose heart the Lord opened,. . .
        Acts 16:14

If you need a new start, God can give you a new heart. Have you undergone God's miraculous open-heart surgery?

31   ## *PROMISE OF HEAVEN*

Beloved,. . .when He shall appear, we shall be like Him;. . .
        I John 3:2

God has so much love for His Son, He wants to fill Heaven with people just like Him.

$\mathcal{A}$ UGUST

1

PROMISE FOR SERVICE

. . .Whom shall I send, and who will go for us? Then said I, Here am I; send me.

Isaiah 6:8

The Lord delights in the little things His children do for Him, as much as He does the big things. Gideon's 300 were better than his original 32,000. Just make what you have available.

2

PROMISE OF A CROWN

And, behold, I come quickly; and my reward is with me, to give every man according as his work shall be.

Revelation 22:12

God has promised His faithful witnesses that

they shall one day. . ."receive a crown of glory that fadeth not away" (I Peter 5:4).

| 3 |

PROMISE OF THE GOLDEN RULE

Therefore all things whatsoever ye would that men should do to you, do ye even so to them. . .

Matthew 7:12

This is known as the Golden Rule, but it doesn't work when we think it applies only to others and not to us. The only way it can work is for everyone to keep it.

| 4 |

PROMISE OF FRUIT

. . .Except a corn of wheat fall into the ground and die, it abideth alone. . .

John 12:24

Fruit bearing comes by dying, not by doing!

| 5 |

PROMISE OF LOVE

By this shall all men know that ye are My disciples, if ye have love one TO another.

John 13:35

If you only have love one FOR another and never get it TO him it will do him no good. With love you have to walk your talk.

6 PROMISE TO SAVE

. . .They that are whole have no need of the physician, but they that are sick. . .

Mark 2:17

The Pharisees, like thousands still, were not sin-sick, but self-satisfied. The self-righteous never like to plead their own cause before God. God will have mercy on sick sinners.

7 PROMISE FOR LIFE

. . .without Me ye can do nothing.

John 15:5

Christ is the Living One, and is come that we might have life. We never look for fruit from a dead tree. A soul dead in sin can never bring forth the fruits of righteousness.

8 PROMISE OF PRAISE

I will praise Thee. . .

Psalm 119:7

To this end we are created. Praise Him continually.

9 PROMISE FOR OBEDIENCE

. . .And he answered and said, I go,. . .

Matthew 21:30

Repentance always precedes the doing of the will of God. Those who go willingly into God's service will find grace sufficient and a holy joy in pleasing Him.

10 PROMISE OF HIS COMING

. . .unto them that look for Him shall He appear the second time. . .

Hebrews 9:28

You can fall asleep while waiting, but you must be awake to LOOK!

11 PROMISE TO CONTINUE

. . .If ye continue in My Word, then are ye My disciples indeed.

John 8:31

If you continue in the love of His Word, you will continue in the power of His Word.

12 PROMISE OF GRACE

Now in the place where He was crucified there was a garden. . .

John 19:41

With every cross you bear there will be a garden of His grace.

13   PROMISE OF SCRIPTURE

All scripture is given by inspiration of God, and is profitable. . .
II Timothy 3:16

The better you know the Author, the more you will love His Book.

14   PROMISE FOR SALVATION

. . .Sirs, what must I do to be saved?
Acts 16:30

This is the world's most important question. The answer is, "Believe on the Lord Jesus Christ, and thou shalt be saved!"

15   PROMISE TO THE POOR

For ye have the poor always with you; . . .
Matthew 26:11

When we count out blessings the poor are made to feel very rich! If it was no disgrace for Jesus to be poor, you should not be ashamed if you have little of this world's goods.

16 PROMISE FOR COMPASSION

And when the Lord saw her, He had compassion on her, and said unto her, Weep not.

Luke 7:13

Our Savior had a tender, loving heart of compassion. Can this be said about you?

17 PROMISE OF JOY

These things have I spoken unto you,. . .that your joy may be full.

John 15:11

The world offers men "pleasures" (Hebrews 11:25), but true joy is found only in Christ. Pleasure depends on things and circumstances. Joy is a grace from the Holy Spirit.

18 PROMISE FOR REST

Come unto me, all ye that labour and are heavy laden, and I will give you rest.

Matthew 11:28

"Come" is one of the sweetest words in the Bible. He gives rest to the heavy laden by His precious blood.

19 PROMISE TO BE WITH US

. . .whose I am, and whom I serve, . . .

Acts 27:23

The more excellent way is not only to work FOR Christ, but to work WITH Him. ". . .If Thy presence go not with me, carry us not up hence" (Exodus 33:15).

20 PROMISE OF PRAYER

Ask, and it shall be given you; seek, and ye shall find; knock, and it shall be opened unto you.

Matthew 7:7

There are three kinds of prayer mentioned in this verse. Asking, seeking and knocking. Insistent "knocking" may be required in some situations. Many people expect a million-dollar answer to a ten-cent prayer.

21 PROMISE OF DELIVERANCE

. . .our God whom we serve is able to deliver us from the burning fiery furnace. . .

Daniel 3:17

If you are willing to brave the oven of man's

wrath to stand up for God and what is right, His help and blessing will be sure.

22 | PROMISE OF THE HOLY GHOST

...*He shall baptize you with the Holy Ghost, . . .*
Matthew 3:11

He is as willing to baptize the saint as to save the sinner.

23 | PROMISE FOR SERVICE

. . .*as ye have done it unto one of the least of these. . .ye have done it unto Me.*
Matthew 25:40

In a practical way you demonstrate your love for Christ by your service to His children.

24 | PROMISE TO THE OVERCOMER

. . .*they overcame. . .by the blood of the Lamb. . .*
Revelation 12:11

God has made provision by His Son, that every child of His should be more than a conqueror (Romans 8:37).

25   *PROMISE OF CONTENTMENT*

. . .I have learned, in whatsoever state I am, therewith to be content.

Philippians 4:11

To temper metals they must be subjected to great heat and cooled slowly, otherwise they become brittle. Paul had been well tempered in the furnace of trial (Psalm 119:71).

26   *PROMISE FOR HEALING*

. . .the Lord shewed him (Moses) a tree, which when he had cast into the waters, the waters were made sweet: . . .

Exodus 15:25

The divinely appointed remedy must be brought into contact with the polluted and bitter waters of life. Man has to take and apply the provided cure. The power of the Savior transforms trials into blessings.

27   *PROMISE OF HIS PRESENCE*

. . .Jesus spake unto them, saying, Be of good cheer; it is I; be not afraid.

Matthew 14:27

He does not at once remove the cause of every

trouble, sometimes He gives rest in the midst
of the storm.

28 *PROMISE FOR RECEIVING*

*. . .What things soever ye desire, when ye pray,
believe that ye receive them, and ye shall have
them.*
                                        Mark 11:24

The supply for every need is at hand. Too
much emphasis cannot be placed upon the
command to "believe that ye shall receive." If
you believe, give thanks.

29 *PROMISE OF EXAMINATION*

*. . .all our righteousnesses are as filthy
rags; . . .*
                                        Isaiah 64:6

Multitudes today endeavor to make their en-
trance to God dressed in the apparel of their
own so-called "good works." Only the works
of the Savior can please the Father.

30 *PROMISE FOR THE LISTENER*

Take heed therefore how ye hear: . . .
                                        Luke 8:18

Careless listening results in much misunderstanding. "He that hath an ear, let him hear what the Spirit saith unto the churches;" (Revelation 2:7)

31   *PROMISE FOR HIS PLEASURES*

. . .thou shalt make them drink of the river of Thy pleasures.

Psalm 36:8

His pleasures are likened to a river, not a stream that can be dried up speedily. His pleasures are forevermore (Psalm 16:11).

SEPTEMBER

1
PROMISE OF RESCUE
. . .underneath are the everlasting arms:. . .
                              Deuteronomy 33:27

The arm of God is a symbol of power. He holds out His arms not only to rescue us from danger, but to satisfy our hearts with love.

2
PROMISE OF GRACE
. . .My grace is sufficient for thee. . .
                              II Corinthians 12:9

It is impossible to grasp the fact that grace is sufficient until we add the first word—MY! Now emphasize the first and last words and

God's grace and our need come together. MY grace is sufficient for THEE!

3   *PROMISE OF DELIVERANCE*

. . .He is able. . .to save them to the uttermost that come unto God by Him,. . .
Hebrews 7:25

Like the Egyptian enemies at the Red Sea, problems may be pressing you today. Tomorrow they will be overwhelmed in the deep (Romans 8:37).

4   *PROMISE FOR HEALING*

For I will restore health unto thee, and I will heal thee. . .
Jeremiah 30:17

Restoration to Himself means health. There are no wounds too deep for His healing power.

5   *PROMISE FOR SALVATION*

. . .I lay down My life,. . .No man taketh it from Me, . . .
John 10:17-18

The voluntary death of Christ was not suicide. A thousand times No! He died for those He came to save. It was not a murder, nor suicide, but a blessed SACRIFICE!

91

6   *PROMISE FOR THE MINISTER*

. . .I have appeared unto thee for this purpose, to make thee a minister and a witness. . .

Acts 26:16

A vessel filled with riches is beautiful. An empty well has no attraction for the thirsty, there is nothing in it but disappointment.

7   *PROMISE OF SERVICE*

They feared the Lord, and served their own gods, . . .

II Kings 17:33

The religion of some folks is like the skin of the chameleon that changes its color according to the circumstances. Let us serve the true and living God.

8   *PROMISE OF JUDGMENT*

. . .The dogs shall eat Jezebel. . .

I Kings 21:23

What a dismal outlook for wealthy sinners! The hope of the wicked shall be cut off (Proverbs 2:22).

9 · PROMISE OF A SONG

For he looked for a city which hath foundations, whose builder and maker is God.

Hebrews 11:10

I don't know what you think about today's so-called "soul music," but real "soul music" is that "new song" which the Lord gives us, which is "praise unto our God."

10 · PROMISE OF WARNING

. . .make not My Father's house an house of merchandise.

John 2:16

To be more concerned about the forms of the Church, than the purpose of the Holy Spirit in the Church, is to introduce a traffic into the holy courts that pollutes and brings dishonor upon the House and Name of God.

11 · PROMISE FOR HEALING

. . .healing all that were oppressed of the devil;. . .

Acts 10:38

Our Lord even heals the wounds sin and Satan have made.

12   *PROMISE OF FAITH*

For he looked for a city which hath foundations, whose builder and maker is God.

Hebrews 11:10

Faith is not satisfied with temples made with hands. Faith seeks eternal realities.

13   *PROMISE FOR GRACE*

. . .we have received grace and apostleship, . . .

Romans 1:5

Grace comes before apostleship. Commitment to the truth comes before commitment to the task.

14   *PROMISE FOR SERVICE*

. . .as for me and my house, we will serve the Lord.

Joshua 24:15

The core of this world is the home. If this heart-center begins to disintegrate, the decay of a nation is sure to follow.

15   *PROMISE FOR PROVISION*

Go to the ant, . . .consider her ways, and be wise.

Proverbs 6:6

94

The ant is unselfish, kind, helping, energetic, searches continually and prepares for the future.

16 PROMISE OF THE FATHER

. . .wait for the promise of the Father, . . .

Acts 1:4

It did not say "work" for the promise of the Father! God can do without your restlessness. The disciples waited, and the filling came.

17 PROMISE FOR SALVATION

For the Son of man is come to seek and to save that which was lost.

Luke 19:10

It is easier to convince a "down-and-outer" of his need for the Savior, than to make a cultured, moral, religious sinner forsake his self-righteousness and repent.

18 PROMISE FOR DELIVERANCE

. . .the Father, . . .hath delivered us from the power of darkness, . . .

Colossians 1:12-13

The greatest freedom that man can know is freedom from sin.

19 — PROMISE FOR DESIRE

. . .the Lord will give you flesh, and ye shall eat. . .until it come out at your nostrils, . . .

Numbers 11:18, 20

God's blessings will never suit the taste of lust. They got what they asked for to such a degree it became a curse. In eternity we may praise God for unanswered prayers.

20 — PROMISE OF SECURITY

. . .I bare you on eagles' wings, and brought you unto Myself.

Exodus 19:4

The path of the eagle is beyond the reach of man. God's way of deliverance is above and beyond the thoughts of men. Christ gave Himself for us that He might bring us to God.

21 — PROMISE OF TRUTH

. . .Master, thou hast said the truth. . .

Mark 12:32

We learn from the Scribes that it is possible to admire the wisdom and character of Christ and yet not enter into the power and blessedness of His life.

22 PROMISE OF THANKS

. . .I thank thee, O Father, . . .

Matthew 11:25

Jesus thanks the Father for two things. First, for hiding these things from the wise. Second, for revealing them unto babes who were willing to receive, trust and be thankful.

23 PROMISE FOR SOUND WORDS

. . .Let no man despise. . . Titus 2:15

Hold fast the form of sound words, . . .

II Timothy 1:13

The fault with faultfinders is the fault they will not face in themselves!

24 PROMISE OF LIVING WATERS

. . .I will give unto him that is athirst of the fountain of the water of life freely.

Revelation 21:6

IT'S FREE! Come and drink of the fountain of perpetual freshness and satisfaction.

25 PROMISE OF FORGIVENESS

. . .I was among the captives. . .the heavens

were opened, and I saw visions of God.

Ezekiel 1:1

It is no use boasting of liberty when we know that our lives are enslaved by lust and sin. The heavens will always open and visions of God be given to those who acknowledge their true state before God and look up for forgiveness.

26   *PROMISE OF PENTECOST*

And when the day of Pentecost was fully come, . . .

Acts 2:1

God's workings are always on time. He's never late, He does nothing prematurely.

27   *PROMISE OF THE SPIRIT*

. . .be filled with the Spirit.

Ephesians 5:18

The Holy Spirit wants to fill the whole man, as the waters fill the sea.

28   *PROMISE OF HIS WORD*

. . .the Word of God, which liveth and abideth forever.

I Peter 1:23

God has made His Word indestructible. It is the one material object that will stand forever.

29   PROMISE OF HEALING

. . .Who healeth all thy diseases.

Psalm 103:3

Every part of man's nature is diseased. Christ will make you whole (I Thessalonians 5:23).

30   PROMISE OF FAITH

. . .faith is the substance of things hoped for, . . .

Hebrews 11:1

Faith acknowledges the things unseen, and acts as if they were visible.

$\mathscr{O}$CTOBER

1
PROMISE TO THOSE ON GOD'S SIDE

. . .*Who is on the Lord's side? let him come unto me.*

Exodus 32:26

Amidst the present confusion there is a great need for stepping out in the Name of the Lord. Those who are not for the Prince of Peace are in the ranks of the prince of darkness. There is no neutrality in this warfare.

2
PROMISE FOR SERVICE

. . .*Then said I, Here am I; send me.*

Isaiah 6:8

The Christian must always be ready for service. God wants your AVAILABILITIES, then He will bless your ABILITIES!

3   *PROMISE OF A SONG*

And when they had sung an hymn,. . .

.Mark 14:26

Jesus sang although the cross was so near. Do you suppose He sang the twenty-third Psalm, "Yea, though I walk through the valley of the shadow of death, I will fear no evil"?

4   *PROMISE OF LOVE*

But the fruit of the Spirit is love. . .

Galatians 5:22

There are nine beautiful graces that make up the cluster of the "fruit of the Spirit."

5   *PROMISE OF CALAMITY*

Because. . .ye refused;. . .I also will laugh at your calamity;. . .   Proverbs 1:24, 26

This is the language of wounded love. His call, His reproof had been fruitless because of the hardness of their heart.

6   *PROMISE TO THE READY*

Be ye therefore ready. . .

Luke 12:40

If Christ is precious to us we cannot but look and long for His personal appearing. Are you ready?

7   *PROMISE OF PROVISION*

But my God shall supply all your need according to His riches in glory by Christ Jesus.

Philippians 4:19

My God, not my job, shall supply all your need, not your greed.

8   *PROMISE FOR THE OBEDIENT*

If ye be willing and obedient, ye shall eat the good of the land.

Isaiah 1:19

The obedient Christian always has a good appetite for spiritual things, and there is plenty to eat!

9   *PROMISE FOR SEPARATION*

Arise ye, and depart; for this is not your rest: because it is polluted, it shall destroy you, even with a sore destruction.

Micah 2:10

The good land given them by the Lord had ceased to be a place of rest for them because of their sin. "Come out from among them, and be ye separate" (Isaiah 52:11).

10

PROMISE FOR SAFETY

. . .How wilt thou do in the swelling of Jordan?"

Jeremiah 12:5

The wise and safe thing to do is to yield yourself to Jesus Christ now, and then, "When thou passest through the waters, I will be with thee; and through the rivers, they shall not overflow thee" (Isaiah 43:2).

11

PROMISE TO SATISFY

Delight thyself also in the Lord; and He shall give thee the desires of thine heart.

Psalm 37:4

It is the nature of love to seek the Lord, and to those who love Him, He will not fail to manifest Himself.

12 | PROMISE FOR PRAYING

But ye, beloved, building up yourselves on your most holy faith, praying in the Holy Ghost.

Jude 20

Praying in the Holy Spirit is a needful, holy and happy labor of love.

13 | PROMISE OF EXPERIENCE

Wherefore glorify ye the Lord in the fires,. . .

Isaiah 24:15

We glorify Him by prayer, singing, walking with Him in the fires and by leaving without the smell of fire.

14 | PROMISE OF LOVE

. . .I love my master,. . .I will not go. . .free:

Exodus 21:5

We love Him because He first loved us. Love is the fulfilling of the law, not duty. May we yield ourselves heartily to the service of the Master.

15 | PROMISE FOR STRENGTH

The eternal God is thy refuge, and underneath

are the everlasting arms:. . .

Deuteronomy 33:27

When you feel that you cannot go another step, take God's almighty arm and He will help you.

16 — PROMISE OF CHEER

. . .sirs, be of good cheer: for I believe God,. . .

Acts 27:25

Only those who believe God's Word will have cheer in the time of ship-wreck.

17 — PROMISE FOR SALVATION

But He was wounded for our transgressions, He was bruised for our iniquities:. . .

Isaiah 53:5

When we think of the cross it is easy to see it as a historical event; but actually we were all participants in the crucifixion. Our sin was laid upon Him.

18 — PROMISE OF RICHES

So is he that layeth up treasure for himself, and is not rich toward God.

Luke 12:21

God has given "unsearchable riches of Christ"

(Ephesians 3:8); to live only for self-interest is to play the fool. "Covet earnestly the best gifts" (I Corinthians 12:31).

19 PROMISE FOR REASONING

Come now, and let us reason together, saith the Lord: . . . Isaiah 1:18
The fact that God offers to reason with us shows His grace does much more abound (Romans 5:20).

20 PROMISE OF AN ANCHOR

Which hope we have as an anchor of the soul, both sure and stedfast, . . . Hebrews 6:19
By laying hold of Jesus as your hope, you are made partakers of His saving power. It is too late to seek the anchor when the ship has split on the rocks.

21 PROMISE OF INCREASE

And the Lord thy God will make thee plenteous in every work of thine hand,. . .
Deuteronomy 30:9
The trees of the Lord's planting take roots downward and bear fruit upward.

22 PROMISE OF SECURITY

. . .neither shall any man pluck them out of My hand. John 10:28

His hand is as gentle as a mother's touch, as strong as the eternal God. We are kept by the grip of Divine power.

23 PROMISE FOR FAITH

Now faith is the substance of things hoped for, the evidence of things not seen. Hebrews 11:1

Substance literally means that which has real existence. Evidence is absolute proof. You can know in your heart that your request has been answered before you see it.

24 PROMISE FOR PEACE

Thou wilt keep him in perfect peace, whose mind is stayed on Thee: . . . Isaiah 26:3

God has given the indwelling Holy Spirit to fortify us and dispel all fear.

25 PROMISE OF WARNING

. . .except ye repent, ye shall all likewise perish. Luke 13:3, 5

Repentance was our Lord's first message in His

107

earthly ministry. It is also His first word to all sinners.

26   *PROMISE OF MERCY*

...the Lord is good; His mercy is everlasting; ...
Psalm 100:5

Could anything be more desirable? His mercy lasts! His truth stands!

27   *PROMISE REGARDING SERVICE*

Neglect not the gift that is in thee, ...
I Timothy 4:14

God gave Moses a rod, David a sling, Samson a jawbone, Dorcas a needle,—and to each the ability to use his gift. Are you using your talent for His glory and the blessing of others? The Lord always gives us what we need to do the job.

28   *PROMISE FOR SALVATION*

Remember Lot's wife.
Luke 17:32

She was outside the city, but her affections were in the city. She was with the right people but that did not save her.

29 PROMISE FOR PROVISION

. . .the ruler of the feast had tasted the water that was made wine. . .　　　　John 2:9

The "best wines" of that day were not the fermented kind, but were sweet and tasty. This was accomplished by slowly simmering the grape juice. "Boiling wines" were non-intoxicating. The heat killed the bacteria and so prevented fermentation. Our Lord, who always provides the best, made only "good wine" (John 2:10).

30 PROMISE FOR FOLLOWING CHRIST

. . .If any man will come after me, let him. . .take up his cross, and follow me.

Matthew 16:24

To bear our cross means the death of self-will and the birth of the God-will for every area of our life.

31 PROMISE OF VENGENCE

Thou hast rebuked the heathen, thou hast destroyed the wicked, . . .　　　Psalm 9:5

All the pride and possessions of the ungodly ". . .shall flow away in the day of His wrath" (Job 20:28).

NOVEMBER

1   PROMISE OF DIRECTION

. . .they left Him, and went their way.

Mark 12:12

In the Word of God there are two ways. We are either on one or the other. The *Broad Way* (Matthew 7:13), or *God's Way* (Acts 18:26).

2   PROMISE FOR HUMILITY

. . .He humbled Himself,. . . Philippians 2:8

"Let this mind be in you, which was also in Christ Jesus" (Philippians 2:5).

3   PROMISE IN HIS NAME

. . .Thy Name is as ointment poured forth,

therefore do the virgins love thee.
Song of Solomon 1:3
There are five marvelous ingredients in the Name of our Lord. ". . .and His name shall be called Wonderful, Counsellor, The mighty God, The everlasting Father, The Prince of Peace" (Isaiah 9:6).

4   PROMISE OF THE GOSPEL
. . .I am not ashamed of the gospel of Christ:. . .
Romans 1:16
Not only is the message good, but the Messenger Himself is All-power and full of Truth.

5   PROMISE FOR THE INQUIRER
They shall ask the way to Zion with their faces thitherward, saying, Come. . .
Jeremiah 50:5
Be honest enough to confess that you do not know the way. Do not be ashamed to take the place of an honest inquirer.

6   PROMISE OF VICTORY
Every place that the sole of your foot shall tread upon that have I given unto you, . . .
Joshua 1:3

There will be Jordans in our path and Jericho walls in our way, but there can be no victory without a planting of the foot of faith.

| 7 |

PROMISE FOR LIFE

. . .that I may dwell in the house of the Lord all the days of my life, to behold the beauty of the Lord, . . .   Psalm 27:4

This was the good part that Mary chose, when she sat at the feet of Jesus. To learn of Him is to behold His glory.

| 8 |

PROMISE CONCERNING SIN

For the bed is shorter than that a man can stretch himself on it: and the covering narrower than that he can wrap himself in it.

Isaiah 28:20

People lie on all sorts of beds of religion and try to cover sin with religious blankets that are too narrow. Uncomfortable sleepers!

| 9 |

PROMISE FOR WISDOM

. . .happy are these thy servants, which stand continually before thee, and that hear thy wisdom.   I Kings 10:8

There are not many to whom this high honor

is conferred. Let us come for a close standing to the King of kings.

10 | PROMISE OF RESTORATION

Instead of which (shields of gold) king Rehoboam made shields of brass, . . .

II Chronicles 12:10

When Rehoboam lost the pure gold what did he do? He made shields of brass. The appearance without the reality. Without love, we become as sounding brass, instead of gold. Let Him restore your soul.

11 | PROMISE TO THE REPENTANT

I will arise and go to my father, . . .

Luke 15:18

This is the language of one whose pride had driven him to the swine. He not only said, "I will arise," but he DID IT!

12 | PROMISE OF THE SPIRIT

. . .I saw the Spirit descending from Heaven like a dove, . . .

John 1:32

The same is true today, the dove-like Spirit comes from an "opened Heaven," and is accompanied with the assuring voice of the Father.

13   PROMISE TO HEED

Unstable as water, thou shalt not excel; . . .
                                    Genesis 49:4
Water appears in unexpected places, like unstable souls.

14   PROMISE FOR CLEANSING

Thy word have I hid in mine heart, that I might not sin against thee.   Psalm 119:11
The new morality really isn't new. It is only the old immorality! The new morality as well as the old immorality are both deviations from the true morality. "Wherewithal shall a young man cleanse his way? . . ." asks the Psalmist; to which he supplies the answer: ". . .by taking heed thereto according to thy word." (Psalm 119:9).

15   PROMISE FOR PEACE

Therefore being justified by faith, we have peace with God through our Lord Jesus Christ.
                                    Romans 5:1
When Christ rules your heart you will have

peace with God. Christians live in peace, others in pieces.

16   PROMISE FOR BELIEVING

But Peter continued knocking: and when they had opened the door, and saw him, they were astonished.   Acts 12:16

Peter had a harder time getting into the prayer meeting than he did getting out of jail. When you pray, believe.

17   PROMISE OF WARNING

. . .the axe head fell into the water: . . .
      II Kings 6:5

It is possible for a Christian worker to lose his sharp edge of power for service. He becomes helpless for effective work. You will find your lost power at that place where you failed to depend on the Holy Spirit, and went on in your own wisdom and strength.

18   PROMISE FOR PRAYER

. . .behold, he prayeth,   Acts 9:11

Saul had frequently said his prayers, but now he prayed.

19 · PROMISE OF SALVATION

Neither is there salvation in any other: for there is none other Name under Heaven given among men, whereby we must be saved.

Acts 4:12

His Name is as a nail in a sure place; it bears all that is hung upon it.

20 · PROMISE OF ETERNAL LIFE

. . .Come thou and all thy house into the ark; . . . Genesis 7:1

Noah and his family obeyed the call; then "the Lord shut him in." So shall it be when the Son of Man cometh—". . .caught up. . .to meet the Lord in the air: and so shall we ever be with the Lord" (I Thessalonians 4:17).

21 · PROMISE OF GOD'S WISDOM

Through faith we understand that the worlds were framed by the word of God,. . .

Hebrews 11:3

If you look at your watch it tells you there must have been a watch maker. When you look outside your window and behold the tree, it tells you there must have been a Creator. God in His wisdom made them all!

116

22 PROMISE OF THANKS

O give thanks unto the Lord; . . .
Psalm 105:1

We need to do more "thanking" and less thinking!

23 PROMISE TO PRAISE

I will praise Thee . . . Psalm 119:7

To this end we are created. Praise Him continually.

24 PROMISE FOR BLESSING

. . .Make this valley full of ditches. . . .that valley shall be filled with water. . .
II Kings 3:16-17

Ditch-digging is a very humble work; but the deeper you dig, the larger the blessing. Prepare ye the way. Make room for God.

25 PROMISE OF THE HARVEST

The harvest is passed, the summer is ended, and we are not saved. Jeremiah 8:20

For the harvest to be "not saved," means the crop is still in the earth. There are so many that have not been harvested. Work while it is day.

26 | PROMISE FOR THE HARVEST TIME

. . .The harvest truly is plenteous, but the labourers are few. Matthew 9:37

A plenteous harvest but a meager labor supply. The solution is twofold, "Pray ye . . . (Matthew 9:38); and "Go ye therefore, . . . (Matthew 28:19).

27 | PROMISE FOR BLESSING

When thou hast eaten and art full, . . .thou shalt bless the Lord thy God for the good land which He hath given thee.

Deuteronomy 8:10

The sufficiency in the good land will satisfy the soul. Let us "bless the Lord" after we have eaten and are full. Fullness of grace makes us thankful.

28 | PROMISE FOR FAITH

But let him ask in faith, nothing DOUBTING (Greek) James 1:6

To doubt what God has promised us in His Word is one of Satan's most effective weapons to rob the believer of peace, healing, joy, spiritual power, blessings and victory. Faith is from God; doubt is from Satan.

29 PROMISE OF SPIRITUAL GIFTS

. . .desire spiritual gifts, . . .

I Corinthians 14:1

He is able and willing to make the greatest possible use of everyone committed to His will. Many complain of fruitlessness, when they are imitating the gifts of others, in the place of desiring spiritual gifts from God.

30 PROMISE OF ETERNAL LIFE

These things have I written unto you that believe. . .that ye may know that you have eternal life, . . .

I John 5:13

When the Lord speaks, we can depend on what He says, for He cannot lie. It's a wonderful thing to have the assurance that you are bound for Heaven. Rely on the facts, not on the feelings.

December

1

PROMISE FOR VICTORY

Submit yourselves therefore to God. Resist the devil, . . .

James 4:7

Resist, don't argue. Resist, don't compromise. Submit and resist, "He will flee from you!"

2

PROMISE FOR MERCY

The Lord taketh pleasure. . .in those that hope in His mercy.

Psalm 147:11

Dare to believe that, behind a frowning Providence, He hides a smiling face.

3

PROMISE FOR PROVISION

. . .Behold, there ariseth a little cloud out of

the sea, like a man's hand.　　　I Kings 18:44
God's "little cloud" can cover your whole sky
and meet all your need (Philippians 4:19).

4　　　PROMISE OF INSTRUCTION
*As they ministered to the Lord, ...the Holy
Ghost said, . . .*　　　Acts 13:2
It is one thing to form plans, and then ask His
guidance; it is quite another thing to trust Him
to form the plans. If we are submissive to Him,
we will be instructed.

5　PROMISE TO THE CALL OF GOD
*. . . .How long wilt thou refuse to humble thyself
before Me? . . .*　　　Exodus 10:3
Many in our own day, like Pharaoh, resist the
call of God. "My Spirit will not always strive
with man, . . ." (Genesis 6:3).

6　　　PROMISE TO THE POOR
*. . . .there is (he) that maketh himself poor, yet
hath great riches.*　　　Proverbs 13:7
Money cannot guarantee happiness. No man
is poorer than he who has allowed earthly
wealth to become his god. God's poor rich

folks have the enduring wealth of Heaven's treasures.

| 7 | **PROMISE OF JUDGMENT** |

. . .but the way of the wicked He turneth upside down. Psalm 146:9

Upside down is a complete change. "The way of the ungodly shall perish" (Psalm 1:6)

| 8 | **PROMISE OF THE RESSURECTION** |

He is not here, but is risen: . . . Luke 24:6

The angels remembered the words that Jesus had spoken, while the disciples had forgotten them. It is easy to forget what we do not really believe.

| 9 | **PROMISE OF THE HOLY GHOST** |

. . .He shall baptize you with the Holy Ghost, . . . Matthew 3:11

He is as willing to baptize the saint as to save the sinner.

| 10 | **PROMISE TO LISTEN** |

. . .He hath inclined His ear unto me. . . Psalm 116:2

What a privilege to have the listening, sympathetic ear of God.

11   *PROMISE OF DELIVERANCE*

This poor man cried, and the Lord heard him, and saved him out of all his troubles.

Psalm 34:6

David found this to be very true by his personal testimony. Our LORD will lend His loving ear to your faintest call.

12   *PROMISE OF GLADNESS*

Serve the Lord with gladness: . . . Psalm 100:2

You would almost think from the tone of some religious meetings that we should serve the Lord with sadness.

13   *PROMISE OF SAFETY*

. . .when I see the blood, I will pass over you, . . .

Exodus 12:13

"When I," not you, "see the blood." Then He assures us of our safety.

14   *PROMISE FOR FAITH*

. . .Have faith in God.

Mark 11:22

God can be trusted to fulfill every promise He has made.

15 PROMISE FOR THE REPENTANT

. . .for I am not come to call the righteous, but sinners to repentance.   Matthew 9:13

God welcomes all who come to repent of their sins. He refuses those who consider themselves "righteous." To be "self-righteous" is as bad as being "unrighteous."

16 PROMISE OF PRAISE

. . .the camp of Judah. . .These shall first set forth.   Numbers 2:9

Judah means "Praise the Lord." Praise leads the way to God. Praise is one of the first signs of a soul truly following the Lord.

17 PROMISE OF THE HOLY SPIRIT

. . .how much more shall your Heavenly Father give the Holy Spirit to them that ask Him?"   Luke 11:13

While Jesus was praying, the Holy Ghost descended (Luke 3:21). When the disciples had prayed, they were all filled with the Holy Ghost (Acts 4:31).

18 | PROMISE OF COMMUNION

. . .the communion of the Holy Ghost, be with you. . . II Corinthians 13:14

When the Holy Spirit is with us, we will be in fellowship with the Father and the Son.

19 | PROMISE FOR SERVICE

. . .Occupy till I come. Luke 19:13

We do not work for our Salvation, but after we are saved God expects us to bring Salvation to the lost.

20 | PROMISE OF PROTECTION

Keep me as the apple of the eye, hide me under the shadow of Thy wings, . . . Psalm 17:8

The strength and carefulness of God are more than enough to save us from our "deadly enemies!"

21 | PROMISE FOR PEACE

. . .having made peace through the blood of His cross. . . Colossians 1:20

This is not a peace made with God, but God-made peace! A peace which the world cannot give.

22 PROMISE FOR FAITH

. . .O thou of little faith, wherefore didst thou doubt?"   Matthew 14:31

When things are going against us and the very foundations seem to be crumbling, how prone we are to forget that our Savior has promised; ". . . I will never leave thee, nor forsake thee." (Hebrews 13:5)

23 PROMISE OF THE SAVIOR

. . .and thou shalt call His name JESUS: for He shall save His people from their sins.

Matthew 1:21

As our Savior He saves us from sin, from self (Galatians 2:20), and from the evil world (Galatians 1:4).

24 PROMISE OF WARNING

. . .I would thou wert cold or hot.

Revelation 3:15

A little girl came home from Sunday school, and her mother asked her to recite the text she had learned: "Many are called but few are chosen." It came out like this: "Many are cold and few are frozen!"

25 PROMISE FOR CHRISTMAS

And when they were come into the house, they. . .worshipped Him:—and. . .presented. . . Him gifts.

Matthew 2:11

Let this day be "glorifying and praising God." Our Savior is worthy indeed. Your greatest possession is your life. Have you yielded it to the Savior. Lay all your talents and ambitions at His feet. They who truly worship Christ will express their adoration by giving themselves.

26 PROMISE OF UNDERSTANDING

I am Alpha and Omega, . . .

Revelation 1:8

Alpha and Omega are the first and last letters of the Greek alphabet. The Lord Jesus is God's alphabet. He is the first and final source of knowledge, understanding and wisdom.

27 PROMISE TO THE WEARY

The eternal God is thy refuge, and underneath are the everlasting arms: and he shall thrust out the enemy from before thee; and shall say, Destroy them.

Deuteronomy 33:27

His arms are everlasting, outstretched and inviting to the weary, much-worn saint. Always, always under, thee to catch and thee to bear.

28   *PROMISE OF PROVISION*

I am the door: by Me if any man enter in, he shall be saved, and shall go in and out, and find pasture.
John 10:9

IN for salvation, worship and renewal; OUT for service, work and revival.

29   *PROMISE OF REFUGE*

Like as a father pitieth his children, so the Lord pitieth them that fear Him.
Psalm 103:13

A little child oppressed by strange alarms, runs swift and straight to father's side. So we, too, throw our troubled selves upon our Father. We cling, and trust in the Lord.

30   *PROMISE OF HIS COMING*

. . .Surely I come quickly. Amen. . .
Revelation 22:20

Three times in this closing chapter of the Bible, the Lord breaks in to remind us that He is

coming quickly. It is only two days to Him (II
Peter 3:8).

31   PROMISE OF DELIVERANCE

*Your adversary the devil, as a roaring lion,
walketh about, seeking whom he may devour:
Whom resist stedfast in the faith.*

I Peter 4:8-9

When we use our faith and authority saying,
"Devil, in the name of Jesus who lives in my
heart, I resist you!" he must flee.